WATERCOLOR PAINTING

A Practical & Easy To Follow Guide For Beginners

Susan Hart

DEDICATION

This book is dedicated to my beautiful and loving girlfriend, Danni.

CONTENTS

Susan Hart

ACKNOWLEDGMENTS

The insights in this book have been passed down to me from a number of inspirational people who I have had the good fortune of meeting. This book could not have been written without you and my life would not be on the path it is now. I am eternally grateful to everybody who has positively impacted my life and I wish to share your wisdom here in these pages through my words. Thank you to all, you know who you are..

DISCLAIMER

No part of this publication may be reproduced or transmitted in any form by any means, mechanical or electronic, including photocopying or recording, or by any information storage and retrieval system, or transmitted by email without permission in writing from the publisher. Reviewers may quote brief passages in reviews.

While all attempts have been made to verify the information provided in this publication, neither the author nor the publisher assumes any responsibility for errors, omissions, or contrary interpretations of the subject matter herein.

This book is for entertainment purposes only. The views expressed are those of the author alone, and should not be taken as expert instruction or commands. The reader is responsible for his or her own actions.

Adherence to all applicable laws and regulations, including international, federal, state, and local governing professional licensing, business practices, advertising, and all other aspects of doing business in the US, Canada, or any other jurisdiction is the sole responsibility of the purchaser or reader.

Neither the author nor the publisher assumes any responsibility or liability whatsoever on the behalf of the purchaser or reader of these

Susan Hart

materials.

Any perceived slight of any individual or
organization is purely unintentional.

A Practical & Easy To Follow Guide For
Beginners

INTRODUCTION

Creating artwork is a beautiful hobby to enjoy. Any form of art embraces a creative connection with how you see the world around you. Painting is an art form that allows you to express your inner thoughts and perspectives through the stroke of a brush. Painting teaches you how to harness the colors in your mind and share them with a canvas.

Not only is painting an excellent skill for your fine motor skills. It is also a proven form of stress relief and has calming attributes that can benefit your life, especially for those of us who have very busy schedules. If you have always felt like an artist on the inside but you have never really known how to release the feeling within, then this book is here as a guide for beginners wanting to learn how to become an artist at home.

This quick and simple guide will focus on the art of painting with watercolors and how you can develop your own style. Unlike other paints, watercolors can be modified in terms of depth and vibrancy depending on how much water you mix in. Through this book, you will learn how simply adding water to a dab of paint and touching brush to canvas can provide you with endless ways of creating breathtaking images to gaze upon.

While staring at a blank canvas can be daunting and unnerving, rest assured that after reading this guide you will have the right technical direction for your painting inspiration to begin.

CHAPTER 1

WHERE TO START: EQUIPMENT

With any new challenge you set for yourself, getting started is always the hardest part. It can be overwhelming know just where to begin. Fortunately, with painting, the simple fact that you are interested in learning is the perfect starting place. Having inspiration and motivation to take up this challenge is exactly what you need. After this, it is time to turn your attention to the resources you need. After all, you need a brush to bring out the images in your mind!

The following list is a general guideline as to what you will need to get started with your watercolor adventure. Remember that this list isn't extensive and it is more or less up to you and what you want to create as to what you will need.

- **Paper:** watercolor suitable paper can be found in pads, individual sheets, or on a canvas. When starting out, it is a good idea to have a sketchpad of watercolor paper so that you can experiment with your ideas and have plenty of paper easily accessible.

As your progress, using individual sheets and a canvas are ideal for working on long-term projects. Watercolor paper has a unique texture and it varies on each side. One side is generally rougher with larger holes for the paint to settle in, and the other side is slightly smoother. Feel both sides and see which texture you prefer to work with.

- **Paint:** you can buy watercolor paints in two forms, either in a tube or a pan. The advantage to the tube is that you can squeeze out as little or as much paint onto the palette as you need at the time. When beginning, it can be a good idea to purchase both and have them both available so you can see which one you prefer.

Warm Colors:
French Ultramarine Blue
Cadmium Red
New Gamboge
Burn Sienna

Cool Colors:

Cerulean Blue

Alizarin Crimson

Lemon Yellow

- **Brushes:** there are a variety of shapes and sizes that watercolor brushes come in. They can be made from synthetic materials or natural. To start off your brush collection, having a small round brush as well as a larger angled flat brush and a big flat brush for washes is an ideal starting point. These are the three main types of brushes that will allow you to experiment with different strokes.

-**Palette:** this is an ideal device for mixing paints. You can start with just the primary colors and mix them to create new colors. A palette is an easy way to keep the mixing process organised. Likewise, the palette is useful in keeping your painting process smooth and organised. There is nothing worse than when you are inspired to paint a stroke and you have to pause to squeeze the paint out of the tube. Having colors pre-arranged on the palette is more convenient. Naturally, the paint can dry out when left overnight. Therefore, having a palette with a lid or some type of cover can preserve you paints and have them ready to use after a long amount of time.

CHAPTER 2

FINDING COLORS: HOW TO MIX WATERCOLOR PAINT

When you start with a palette of watercolors in the primary colors, you are in fact looking at a whole rainbow waiting to be mixed. Watercolors are unique in the sense that they can be blended and toned to make many different colors and shades.

With watercolors paints, each colour tends to have multiple different shades. This opens up many possibilities for being able to mix colors and create many new colors. When faced with the choice of so many different colors in a store, it can be difficult to know which ones to get.

The best base colors for a paint collection include:

- **Primary colors** are the colors you use to create more colors. These consist of *red, yellow, and blue*. Watercolor paints come in different shades, such as cool and warm as shown in the table above. This range of cool and warm gives more options when mixing colors. For example, you can take a cool blue and mix it with yellow to create a lighter shade of green. Likewise, a warm red can mix with a warm blue and create a dark, vibrant purple.

- **Secondary colors** are the colors that are mixed by two primary colors together. These include *violet/purple, orange, and green*. You can then take a primary colour and mix it with a secondary colour to have more colour and tone options.

- **Complementary colors** are colors that are opposite to each other. For example, blue and yellow are mixed to make green. Red is not used in this mix; so red is therefore the complementary colour of green. Similarly, red and yellow are mixed to make orange. Blue is not used in this mix, so blue is complementary to orange.

Complementary colors are handy to keep in mind because they create harmony to a colour scheme. Once you understand which colors best complement each other, try to use them side-by-side in your paintings to gain a harmonised balance in the artwork. After some time experimenting with colors and mixing, it will become natural to choose the best colors to paint beside each other in a piece.

CHATER 3

BASIC TECHNIQUES AND TOP TIPS TO REMEMBER

Painting is a very liberal hobby in that there is no correct way to paint. We all see the world differently and have unique perspectives. Painting allows you to express your individuality and show the world how you see. This means that it is essentially impossible to paint incorrectly.

However, there are some techniques that can assist you in finding you watercolor painting style. These techniques relate mostly to the way you hold the brush and the type of strokes you can create with different brushes for a variety of effects while painting.

- **Flat wash**

This is when you use a large, flat brush to create a smooth and even layer of paint. You do this by wetting the brush with water and paint and then move the brush along in a quick movement across the canvas. This technique doesn't need too much pressure, rather a gentle application to get the right affect.

- **Wet canvas**
The use of water creates beautiful effects in watercolor painting. For this technique, use a sponge or spray bottle to wet the canvas, then use the wet brush with paint on it to colour the area. Painting over the damp surface will create a beautiful, blurry look, which is great for characterising backgrounds.

- **Dry brush**
For smaller and refined elements of the image, using a dry brush can give precedence to crisper details. Using a dry brush allows details, particularly in the foreground, to stand out against the wetter background and larger strokes of the image.

- **Soften the edges**
To create gradient blurs and soft edges on your canvas, this is a great technique. To

achieve this is take a clean paintbrush and wet it. Use this to trace over the lines you want to soften immediately after you have painted them. The water will blur the colors of the lines together and make it look soft and feathered.

CHAPTER 4

BRUSH TO CANVAS: BRUSH STROKE TECHNIQUES

When it comes to painting, the world is literally your oyster in that there is a blank canvas waiting for your touch to come to it. There are many ways that you put brush to canvas to create images, shades, tones, and expression. Watercolor painting is very flexible and can be done with the finest brush tip to large, flowing strokes.

When painting watercolors, it is important to pay attention to how you are holding the brush. Watercolor painting doesn't require much brush pressure as it a very fluid form of fine art. Therefore you don't need to hold the brush too tightly. It is better to hold the brush loosely towards the top of the handle and gently put it to the canvas.

Some effective brush strokes to practice include:

- **Stippling** is ideal for creating leafy trees or flowers and bushes with texture. It is done using a flat brush and holding it very lightly, dap the paint onto the paper repeatedly in the same area.

- **Lining** is when you want to create thinner, finer strokes, like the branches or a tree or details of a human body. A fine tip brush is needed for this. Holding the brush at the top of the handle, gently apply the brush to the canvas and move the brush in the desired direction.

- **Angling** involves using a flat brush and applying the paint at an angle. Here you take the broad, flat brush and touch the flat edge to the canvas, then slowly move the brush and twist it. This will create an angled effect, which can add depth to elements of a picture like leaves and clouds.

CHAPTER 5

ADD SOME DEPTH: HOW TO BLEND AND SHADE

The most breathtaking paintings are ones that have depth and character in the canvas. Watercolor painting gives you the chance to add layers to the image you are painting by blending and shading. This is a technique that can be applied in a whole variety of ways when using watercolors and a canvas.

You have many options on how to blend and shade watercolor paints. Some choices you can try out include:

- **Charging colors,** which involves mixing watercolor paints directly on the canvas. Rather than mixing the colors in a palette, you can blend two colors together by using a clean, wet brush and blurring the line edges together.

- **Spray water** on thick paint areas. To do this, start by having some paint mixed with only a small amount of water to make it thick. Apply it to the canvas. Then use a spray bottle to spread and lighten the paint. You can then use the brush to ensure the colour goes where you want it. This technique adds texture to blending.

- **Use a sponge** to create smooth transitions between colors. This can be done either by having separate paint colors in the palette and using the brush to apply a line of each colour onto the wet sponge. Then press the sponge onto the canvas and move it slowly. This can create a stunning ombre effect. Alternatively, you can use a clean, damp sponge to blend the colors once they are already on the canvas and create a blurred, blended effect between colors in the image.

- **Shading** is best done by layering the colors. Starting with a base layer, leave it to dry. Then build on the layers, adding depth and shading to places in the image that need to be darker. You can also do shadowing in this same manner to add a three dimensional effect to an image where desired.

- **Dripping** the paint is an effective way to blend colors. For example, when painting a skyline, start by painting a thick line of blue at the top of the canvas. Stand the canvas upright and take a clean, wet brush and run it along the paint. The colors will then run down the canvas. To add more texture, move the canvas around and shift the paint to create a dynamic sky.

CHAPTER 6

EXPERIMENT AND FIND YOUR OWN

Watercolor painting is beautifully frustrating in that there is absolutely no right or wrong way to do it. From fine and detailed paintings to loose impressionistic masterpieces, watercolor is a style of painting that you can make entirely your own. Of course, this is often easier said than done when you are faced with such endless ways to fill the canvas with colour.

Here are some ideas on how you can get inspiration to begin your experimentation:

- **Paint a photograph:** flick through your photos and see if there is a landscape of photo that you really like. Starting with scenic images can be an easy to get started as they are generally easily divided into a background and foreground. Having the photographic image beside you while you paint can help keep you on track and

envisage how you want the finished
product to look.

- **Paint different subjects:** still working
  with photographs, try painting different
  subjects. For example, after a landscape
  photo, find a photo of a flower, an animal,
  even a person, and try painting the
  photograph.

- **Paint what you are passionate about:**
  the best way to keep your motivation alive
  is to paint something you love. If you have
  a favourite painting, try to recreate it in
  watercolor. If you love animals, paint your
  pets. If you love the beach, paint the
  ocean. The more passion you put into
  your painting, the better the result will be.

After some time experimenting with different
images, landscapes, settings, or anything else you
choose to paint, you will begin to get a feel for
what style you are most comfortable with. The
general rule of thumb with anything arty is to
follow your heart and create what makes you
happy.

CONCLUSION

Hopefully throughout reading this guide you have felt inspiration to test out some new techniques and styles with your watercolor painting. The purpose of this is not to instruct you on what you paint or the exact manner to hold your brush, but rather to encourage you to paint with feeling and individuality – this is what makes the best paintings. So the last thing to do is grab your paintbrush, mix up some colors, and release your inner thoughts onto the canvas. Take a step back and you'll feel proud and impressed with what you can achieve with a paintbrush in hand!

THE END…

ABOUT THE AUTHOR

Susan is a professional author, a life coach and a lifelong student of holistic and alternative medicine. Some of her biggest passions in life are: yoga, meditation, health and vitality, teaching, coaching and giving.

Her purpose in life is to grow and advance myself as a person so that she can better help people transform their lives by sharing and giving back to them the knowledge and wisdom she has picked up.

She lives every day with clarity and peace. She meditates. She workouts. She eats healthy and clean (usually she has 1 cheat day a week... that's the only way she can be consistent). She uses essential oils every day for every part of her life to ensure she is operating at the highest level she can possibly be. She is passionate about sharing all these experiences and the expert knowledge she has accumulated over the years with the world and aims to deliver as much value to as many people as possible. This is what has led her to writing her books. If you have read any of her books, she truly hopes they have added value to your life and she thanks you with all her heart for trusting in her.

Outside of being an author, she works as a personal trainer & life coach. Employing her deep knowledge of alternative treatments has enabled her to provide outstanding results for all of her clients!

In her spare time you will often find her lounging in her hammock reading the latest aromatherapy magazine or romantic fiction novel. She has a soft spot for true romance! She aims to meditate at least once a day, and practice yoga 5 times a week. Her biggest hobby however is exploring the beautiful world that we live in. Next on her hit list is Palawan, there is something seriously alluring about that island.

Thanks for reading.

www.ingramcontent.com/pod-product-compliance
Lightning Source LLC
Chambersburg PA
CBHW070428190526
45169CB00003B/1466